T0196719

THE
WORLD
IN MY EYES

RACHENZA PROSPER

THE WORLD IN MY EYES

iUniverse books may be ordered through booksellers or by contacting:

iUniverse
1663 Liberty Drive
Bloomington, IN 47403
www.iuniverse.com
1-800-Authors (1-800-288-4677)

Because of the dynamic nature of the Internet, any web addresses or links contained in this book may have changed since publication and may no longer be valid. The views expressed in this work are solely those of the author and do not necessarily reflect the views of the publisher, and the publisher hereby disclaims any responsibility for them.

Any people depicted in stock imagery provided by Thinkstock are models, and such images are being used for illustrative purposes only. Certain stock imagery © Thinkstock.

ISBN: 978-1-5320-2372-9 (sc)
ISBN: 978-1-5320-2373-6 (e)

Library of Congress Control Number: 2017909594

Print information available on the last page.

iUniverse rev. date: 07/22/2017

ACKNOWLEDGMENTS

This book has developed me as a person, and I will admit I gave up more times than I can count. But I knew that writing this book will not only change my life but someone else's too. I want this book to help others see things differently and be more open minded with life and struggles at hand.

Thanks to:

MY MOM RACHEL. Without my mom's help I wouldn't have been able to create this book, so thank you mom for giving me this chance of expressing myself to the world. Even though you didn't know till later that I had such great passion to write poems, but you still took the risk of spending money for me to do something big in my life. That means so much to me.

My family for supporting me and promising to get a copy to support me through this big accomplishment.

My ELA teacher Ms.Falcone, without her great editing skills I would not be able to express myself in proper grammar. You were a great support and it means a lot to me that you took time out of your day to help edit this wonderful book.

Also wanna shout out my friends who help inspired me to write certain poems.

This is my first book and I couldn't have wrote it any other way, so please enjoy reading and seeing the world in my eyes.

I also would like to thank my father for also giving support through this process in the way that he can.

CONTENTS

Part I
Surroundings

Part II
Beauty

Part I

SURROUNDINGS

FROZEN IN TIME

I'm stuck in a time,
where I have no control
no emotions are even shown.
If maybe I tried I could move and
leave this time.
But I've given up on hope and even
my pride.

I'M NOT KEEPING QUIET

They had shackles on their arms,
Shackles on their legs.
Shackles on their hearts, holding pain and horrible regret.
The sweat running down their bodies,
Couldn't wash away the filth.
The scars and bruises on their bodies,
Never faded and never healed.
There's no lie in the saying that life was in black and white.
The one's you call your ancestors know exactly why.
Living in a time where being black is poison,
And being white enough is a promotion.
We will never understand the feeling of being a save.
Or being treated like an animal ,
throughout your whole life and day.
See now where living comfortable,
Everything comes our way.
Unlike your ancestors you've never been caged away.
We thought the hatred on our skin color has gone away,
But now here we go again with
bullets going through our brains.
I know this an issue that tends to be closed away,

But I'm not keeping quiet.
Not till the cops stop shooting away,
I'm not keeping quiet till the president sees it our way.
And I'm not keeping quiet till the young ones realize,
That the color they are is more of a prize than a mistake.
I'm not keeping quiet till the chains that
holds us back are broken away.
I'm not saying this to shame the white, or even hurt feelings.
I'm opening your eyes to the reality hidden away.

LIFE

We eat, we bathe
We talk and save
we travel to big cities,
Carrying big dreams and pity.
New life is created,
And life will be taken.
This is our lives,
Nothing more nothing less.

CAFE

So small yet cozy,
With the light smell of coffee
Small tables and seats,
Young teens coming just to eat
Desserts that make you feel at peace.
Different flavors of sweetness,
Making you wish your grandma could bake it.
The cafe is your home,
Made out of your community.

OCEAN WAVES

Blue like crystal,
Soft sounds like whistles.
Gives inner peace,
With good vibes.
The only place that'd cheer you up,
When you cry,
Or even hurting with pain or happy with good days.
The ocean will always be there floating the negativity away.

PURSUE IN HAPPINESS

In life they prepare you for one goal,
Success.
They tell you to try your best,
And put all your effort
So that you may achieve what you do best.
But they don't tell you
to do what makes you happy
To enjoy your talent,
and take risk even though they may not pass.
They tell you to do what will get food on the table,
What will put a roof over your head.
But won't doing what makes you happy,
Come with all that is needed.
Why waste your time doing what only gives you money?
But does not fur fill your life with happiness.

BLACKBIRD

So small and lonely,
With the aroma of danger.
It'll never know to love,
But will always know to fly.
No one understands it,
No one seems to care why.
Its alone with no care,
Yet it doesn't care.
As long as it has wings to fly,
It'll be happy in the inside.

COMA OF DREAMS

You fall into darkness,
Yet you feel protected.
The images are slow
The movement of your body feels like,
Your trapped and under snow.
Numb.
The voices are silent,
In your eardrums.
You want to reach out and touch the owner
Of the voice,
But the dream wraps it's arms around you.
suffocating you back into darkness.

TRAVEL

We go on and on
Around the globe.
Wondering where to go next,
And what our next destination holds.
Meeting new friends creating new adventure,
Until the world looks like one big picture
The meaning of travel is knowing the
world at the back of your hands.
Expanding your community,
While it stands.

POETRY TO ME

They may be words to you,
But they aren't to me.
Because I see it differently.
I'm able to open my mouth,
And speak fluently.
Say what I want to say and be who I want to be,
Each phrase each letter means more to me.
So yes there is more to poetry,
It's not just words and its not just a piece of paper.
It's opening myself to the world,
And seeing it to be better.
This isn't an exact definition,
There's more to it out there.
But this is poetry to me.

SOCIETY SUCKS

See in this world,
We're all separated.
It may seem like were united,
But were really just divided.
In order to hang with certain people,
You must be like those people.
Society makes it look like,
Being different is accepted.
Yet people are always put down for,
Not being like someone else.
And its been put into our heads,
That we must always "fit".
That we must dress or think,
Like the cool ones.
Or the popular ones.
The people that are being acknowledge the most.
But you don't need to be like someone else to feel,
Being yourself is actually the best part in a person.

LOOK IN THE INSIDE

When you see a person you see the outside of them,
You see the door.
Some may have locks some may not even have a door knob,
But its still the outside of the door.
Sometimes you're afraid to enter or
sometimes they don't want you to,
But its just the outside of the door and the door isn't important,
Its about what inside.
So don't judge someone so quickly if
you've never been past that door.

POSITIVITY

We talk about it all the time,
Asking yourself why don't you spread it a few times.
We ask of it from others we share it with each other,
But still the world is dying even faster.
If only we'd spread it more than 3 or 5 times,
The world would have been smiling.
Glady it's not too late so spread positivity today,
Spread it so much you lose count,
So much that you can't stop smiling.

IF ONLY

If only she had the voice to yell out to those who told her,
Size will always matter no matter the person.
If only she had the voice to yell out to those who told her,
being her skin color will push her back in life.
If only she had a voice to yell out to those who told her,
beauty has no reflection towards her name.
If only she had the voice.
We all were born with a voice and so was she.
So she stands up tall and yells out,
I am who I want to be no matter the size,
no matter the color and beauty will always reflect in me.

LABELS

We weren't born into the world
With them.
But somehow the labels follow within,
You hear it so much you accept it.
Thinking this is who I am,
And there's no changing it.
But let's be honest if you were born into the world,
With no name no label just you.
Who would you be, what would
you name it and how would you be it.
The world thinks that being labeled is an important thing,
That being this or that,
Is better than other things.
It may be true but most labels were just given to you,
If I were to stand up and name myself what I want,
I would be called so many names,
But don't let fear take over you take a stand now
knowing that labels just aren't for you.

MY LIFE

Another day,
Another mistake.
But yet somehow I look forward to it all,
Waiting for the day when I'll recall all my mistakes,
As the wounds I've fought.

DON'T SHOOT

Once those two hands go up,
All you hear is,
Silence.
Not one pin drop,
Not one drag of air.
Silence.
Don't shoot,
The words slip out,
With hope and truth.
Pockets empty,
Yet soul feels heavy.

IF ONLY I COULD FLY

If only I could fly,
I could spread my wings.
Letting all the hatred,
And enemies fall behind.
There'd be peace and,
Comfort and all that I need to flap my
Wings all the way to the sky.
If only I could fly.

THROUGH THE EYES

Through the eyes,
Lays a story.
With a surprise and one tear of worry.
Through the eyes,
I see hope and doubt.
When smiling, the eyes shine brighter than the stars.

THE WORDS I NEVER SAID TO MY MOM

Hugging you makes my day,
Your fragrance giving me a sense of safety.
I actually love it when you brag about me to your friends,
Letting me know my accomplishments,
Mean quite a lot to you than it does to me.
You no you longer have your mother,
But the thought of losing you is death to me.
When I reach my success you'll be the number one person,
I dedicate all my hard work to.
I may not show it, but you know it. I love
you from the moon and back.

SUNSET

The colors pink,
And orange in the sky.
Creates a warmth inside,
My cold heart.
Gives me a feeling of,
Home and comfort.
If there was a way,
Id lock you away.
To look up at you,
On my bad days.

THE GIRL BEHIND
THE CAMERA

When she sees the light,
Its only the flash of the camera in her eyes.
Big smile, no frowns.
Sucked in stomach, no fat for the world to comment
When the camera isn't up in her face,
She's at home browsing through the comments of hate.
Her only goal is to impress the fans,
Yet the pressure is making her shake her head.
She can't lie to the young girls,
She can't lie to these young girls.
The truth is, she's lying.
Yeah that's right,
The same girl you look up to is hiding in disguise.
She want's you to hide, this world will push you to fake it.
Tell you you're not worth it,
Make you second guess the meaning of perfect.
So Run.
Run until your legs are sore, and you can't feel them anymore.
Don't get caught up in this lie, your beauty is not a prize.
It should never be given away or taken,
It's to be kept away for your eyes to admire
your beauty.

WINTER BABY

She smiles when she's happy,
She smiles when she's sad.
She fears the shadows,
That hover over her head.
She feels happy when she sees snow.
The joy of Christmas feels like home.
She thrives for the holidays and especially her birthday.
She's may be cold but she's warm in the inside,
She's a winter baby.

SUCCESS

To me it's a prize,
We all want to thrive.
It's never given but must be found.
You have to earn,
And work hard,
For success to be in your life.
And once you have it you won't regret it.
Success is the key to your life.

BOOKS ARE MY LIFE

Every chapter, every page.
Is a prize to me.
Being sucked into a new life,
Feels like freedom.
There will be happiness,
There will be sadness.
Books are my life.

ROSE

Your bright red hair reminds me,
Of a rose that blooms high up in the air.
Your voice as soft and sweet like,
A beautiful melody.
On repeat.
You're there for me when I need you,
And there for me when I hate you.

PHOTO ALBUM

Picture by picture,
More memories gather.
Its not about the moment or about the thought,
But about the people and
the emotion you shared.
And who you enjoyed it with,
Friends and family create the memory,
Even the best strangers.

Part II

BEAUTY

A LETTER TO MY BODY

I always wonder why you hide yourself so far
Into the corner.
I always question the amounts you take in.
I always push you to do the things that
even you know I'll regret.
I can't help but love you even in the tearful nights.
You hug me close and keep me warm at night.
You taught me to love you, whenever I crave to hate you.

HAIR

Sure to you it's just something that's on your head,
And it may be a struggle.
But it's YOUR HAIR it's you it grows with your body,
with a story that only you can tell.
Short hair, long hair, straight hair.
curly hair, red hair, black hair.
blue hair, brown hair, and blonde hair.
No matter the color no matter the size its still your hair.
Even a hairless head has a story.
It's not about it being hair it's about it being
apart of you that makes up the story.

SKIN

You're my shield, you're me.
You express myself, But not so deep.
No matter what you show, no matter what they see.
They may see you, but they don't see what's underneath.
But still, you're my skin.

STICKS AND STONES

You yell, you laugh.
You criticize, while I spit back.
No matter what you say,
No matter what I hear.
I'll always believe in me,
Cause even if you break me.
Your words may never hurt me,
For I am who I am.

MIRROR

So clear, so true.
Yet I may think what is shown is unfair.
And maybe what you hold, is only in my head.
But I know deep down, what I see is the truth.
And what you want me to see is beauty,
And even if I want to change.
I can't change what isn't seen.

CURVES

So smooth, so visible.
You flow in different places,
You defined the beauty of my shape.
You may be odd to others, but I'll always see you as beauty.
You mean more to me than to others,
You show me that I'm maturing in many ways.

COUNTING CALORIES

The numbers haunts our dreams,
always worrying if we've had too much,
or just not enough.
But just cause we count,
Does not mean we'll feel better.
Because if we are losing,
How are we gaining in beauty.
So stop counting and just start living.

1-10

Who would want their beauty
to be scaled by a number.
Not even the numbers between 1 and 10,
Can define beauty itself.
No matter the gender or difference,
beauty is so well defined that
not even a number in existence,
Could label it.
There's not one person who's beauty
is in between numbers 1-10.
Their beauty are xfinity and beyond,
It's impossible to label.

SCARS

Its marked you for life,
You wish it'd go away, even if it won't.
It may seem ugly and old,
But underneath is a story.
One that shows your strength, Shows
that you're no longer small.
And now you stand tall.
Something you couldn't do before,
If not for that scar you wouldn't be reminded of the reason.
You're no longer weak.

THE GIRL IN THE MAGAZINE

Perfect hair, Small hips.
Long hair, All that you think you need.
All that you wished you have,
But just cause she seems perfect.
Doesn't mean it's true,
No one is perfect.
Beauty is a gift within,
So why would you want to change
When your gift is just as good as hers.

SOCIETY STANDARDS

Society has pushed girls to their lowest,
making it seem like being the way they are is a shame.
But why should we wanna look a certain
way to please someone else than
ourselves,
Beauty isn't about pleasing the others around.
But being comfortable in our skin,
So don't try to look like all the others.
Instead try to look good for you.

HIJAB

She puts her head low,
Scared that just because she wears a hijab
She is not beautiful.
That is a lie,
She's judged for having her beauty hidden
but at least it comes with reason.
And now you can stare at the beauty of her face,
Instead of her hair or her body.
Because she is Muslim she is weak.
That is a lie.
Her history is full of stories of a woman named Malala,
Who fought for something so strong
That a bullet to her head didn't even seem wrong.
She is beautiful she is strong because she represents
and always has her hijab on.

MY DEFINITION
OF BEAUTY

There's a lot more to beauty.
Beauty is being able to stand up for
what is wrong,
And never afraid to be pushed far.
Beauty is being able to say you made it,
Even though they always doubt it.
Beauty isn't always about worrying about looking the best,
But being able to show true confidence.
But the real truth is
Beauty is you.

MEAN GIRLS

They love to talk,
Because they think they're above you.
They give you weird looks,
Making sure you know too.
They put you down,
Making it seem like you need their approval.
But you don't need to be them,
The only reason they stare
Is because they wish they were you.
And being you is actually more better than you think,
Because you are awesome and unique
And that is very rare.
So girls lets stop putting
Each other down.
And stand together accepting each others flaws.

LOST GIRL

We all went through the stage of being a lost girl.
She no longer knows what to believe,
The struggle of inner confidence is a
battle she no longer can win.
She doesn't see the beauty that exists within,
She only believes what she is told.
Negativity is all that flows through her head.
She feels trapped,
And lost.

JUST CAUSE SHE HAS CANCER

She's fighting a big battle bigger than she thinks,
but even with that battle she pushes herself to her best.
just cause she has cancer doesn't mean she lacks in her beauty,
She's strong and beautiful that not even the
lack of hair can put her beauty down.
She may be hurting in the inside but she doesn't let it show,
Beauty isn't all about what's on the
outside, beauty is also strength.
And she is as strong as she can be.

GIRL'S RUN THE WORLD

Guys think we are weak,
But we know we are strong.
We can fight our own battles,
With our own bare hands.
They think less of us,
But because of our ancestors.
We're able to do much more than they think,
And use the knowledge that we have on everything.
We are proud to be girls.
Guys think of us like glass,
That in any moment we'll shatter to pieces.
We know better, we know the meaning,
Of brave and strong.
We know when to fight and when to be soft,
We aren't weak and we sure aren't glass.
Cause unlike glass,
If you push us down we will not break
We'll always get right back up.

TOO THIS OR TOO THAT

She's either too thin,
Or
She's either too thick.
She's either too tall,
Or
She's either too small.
But there is no skinny or fat.
There is no difference,
So what if she's bigger than her
Or even smaller.
So what if her clothes are loose
Or even tight.
Because in the end
her size isn't her personality.
her size isn't her beauty.
Size doesn't define her or anyone.

EXPECTATIONS

Once we're born into this world
There's expectations for us
Though we were too young to notice it was there.
But we did become aware as we grew into the women we are.
The clothes we were expected to wear,
The way we must act.
And what we must eat,
Though we never ask for these expectations.
But we can't leave them,
We were born into it.
But we can have a voice against it,
We should be able to create our own expectations for ourselves.
Its our life and we have a choice,
So speak over those expectations.

IN DISGUISE

We don't want to be judged,
We're scared to be seen as who we are.
So we hide behind a fake mask,
Trying to show the world that It's who you are.
Even when it's not.
We force ourselves,
To act differently,
To please society.
But we're not the typical girls that society wants,
Us girls should stop trying to act.
Like everything about us is all right,
That we live with no flaws.
And that we can always get through it all,
So let's take off our mask and stop hiding in disguise.
Be who you are
flaws and all.

ALL CULTURE

No matter where you came from,
No matter what language you speak.
No matter the skin tone,
You are the definition of beauty.
You may be different,
And we may not all act the same.
But we are all beautiful.
Even through our diversity,
No matter what we have one thing
In common.
Beauty.

THE BEAUTY OF A
BLACK WOMAN

A black girl who doesn't take her skin for granted.
She's able to be the first of,
her color or gender in almost everything.
She's proud of her natural hair,
The form of her body.
And the meaning and history behind,
The beauty of her race.
Knowing that
Every black woman is beautiful.

FAMOUS LOOKS

We all want to look like the latest,
Celebrities.
Wanting to be as popular or beautiful,
As they can be.
They may be famous,
And beautiful.
But they're human too,
And may not see what you see.
It may seem like the looks matter to them,
But deep down it may seem less to them.
We all have insecurities and feelings,
And they do too.
So there's no difference between their beauty and you,
We all have some type of flaw.
So accept it.

ADMIRE

I believe that every girl should be able,
To stand in front of a mirror.
Not letting the negativity get to their heads,
To be able to look at themselves instead.
Stare at what you are gifted with,
Not what you want to change.
Or even what you hate,
But the beauty under your gaze.
Acknowledging what they didn't see before,
Every girl has those things about them that they love.
So look in the mirror and admire,
What's yours.

LOVING YOURSELF

You cannot see yourself as beautiful, if you don't believe its true.
You can't have the self confidence of your beauty,
if you don't see what is needed to see.
You must open your mind to accepting,
who and how you are.
Without taking any part of your body for granted or a mistake.
You must love yourself from head to toe.
Before you can walk around knowing and,
Understanding that you have all the beauty needed.
And that you aren't missing one piece.

THE LOOK

They gaze with hard eyes,
Looking up and down they never seem to miss a spot.
Their looks always have a meaning behind it.
Once you see the smirk on their lips,
Or how they turn to their friends to gossip.
They just can't seem to realize that none of us are perfect,
That if they can find many flaws in us we
can find just as many in them.
We shouldn't let their negativity,
Jump off to us.
Because its sad of them to put you down,
When we all have flaws.
So don't pass on negativity but positivity,
Cause how would you feel
if the roles were reversed.

DON'T EVER BRING
YOURSELF DOWN

No matter what others may say about you,
Or even think of you.
Don't ever let their opinions take over your mind,
Of thinking its true.
If what they say of you is negative than they
Themselves don't understand the beauty within you.
So always let the negative fly out your ears,
And think of the real truth of your beauty.
That just cause you hear it doesn't make it true,
And that no matter what.
You are beautiful.

"The World in My Eyes so clear to see, so hard to believe. So I write it down and share my rants and motivations for girls like me."

ABOUT THE AUTHOR

Rachenza Prosper is currently a high school student who has been writing since she was a child. She lives with her mother in Boston, Massachusetts. This is her first poetry collection.

Printed in the United States
By Bookmasters